SOMETIMES MUSIC RISES

SOMETIMES MUSIC RISES

Poems by Wayne Dodd

THE UNIVERSITY OF GEORGIA PRESS

ATHENS AND LONDON

© 1986 by Wayne Dodd
Published by the University of Georgia Press
Athens, Georgia 30602

Designed by Betty McDaniel
Set in 10 on 13 Linotron 202 Bembo

The paper in this book meets the guidelines for
permanence and durability of the Committee on
Production Guidelines for Book Longevity of the
Council on Library Resources.

Printed in the United States of America

90 89 88 87 86   5 4 3 2 1

Library of Congress Cataloging in Publication Data

Dodd, Wayne, date.
Sometimes music rises.

I. Title.
PS3554.O32S66   1986   811'.54   85-16533
ISBN 0-8203-0823-4 (alk. paper)
ISBN 0-8203-0824-2 (pbk. : alk. paper)

ACKNOWLEDGMENTS

The author and the publisher gratefully acknowledge the following publications, in which some of these poems first appeared, sometimes in slightly different form.

The Chariton Review: "And If Someone . . . ," "Beside Mill Creek," "Driving the School Bus," "Some Mornings When I Wake," and "Two Love Poems."
The Denver Quarterly: "And What Shall We Gather to Us."
The Georgia Review: "Before Divorce," "Of Butterflies," "On All Your Fingers," "Sometimes Music Rises," and "Tongues."
The Iowa Review: "Again" and "Two Winter Poems."
The Kansas Quarterly: "November."
The Nation: "Of Rain and Air."
The Ontario Review: "Deer Tracks in March."
Raccoon: "Love Poem as Meditation."
The Southern Review: "Nags Head."
West Branch: "Glacier Trail: Rainbow Trout."
Willow Springs: "Down the Many Steps of Light."

The publication of this book is supported by a grant from the National Endowment for the Arts, a federal agency.

FOR STANLEY PLUMLY

CONTENTS

I

II

III

. . . *because truly being here is so much; because everything here apparently needs us, this fleeting world, which in some strange way keeps calling to us. Us, the most fleeting of all.*

Rilke

I

TWO WINTER POEMS

Beside the creek potentilla
bushes grow
like boulders, dark
with the absence of flowers.
White and green only
this landscape.
But from the vanished
rafters of a porch,
flycatchers dart into spring
like necessary
yellow, bright in the eyes.

*

Freezing, even beneath thick
blankets: *These two hundred
bones will grow cold
strangers to themselves.*
In the long chill of dreams we listen
to the snap of pine cones ticking open
above us, like logs
on fire with the future.

OF BUTTERFLIES

There can be no doubt, the same
one, come back for the ninth
day in a row to the boards
beside me: the small tear
in the wing tip, the curved
line in the opened
wings, like a horseshoe's brown
shape stamped strangely
on the earth, antennae
sifting the air
for messages.

*

What is it that brings it
always back
to this spot
and me? like an image
of my mother, standing small
and bright in the summer
grass, raising her arms
from the shoulders
of the light voile dress my
father gave her
on her birthday . . .

*

You walk down a familiar road one day
in August, the sun setting
behind you, the light wind cooling your chest

and arms. The trees are beginning to give up
the light they held all day
in their leaves, and cicadas rasp to a stop
along the branches.
Then, for an instant,
on top of a fence post,
a man you've never seen
before appears, soft hat pushed
back from his forehead,
one leg swinging
down, arm raised
in greeting.
And as you sit
to supper,
a bluebird, in the last
clarity of light outside,
darts again and
again against the window.

*

Thus young men pack their bags
one morning and catch a train
to a city they've never been to,
or else walk off
with only change in their pockets,
certain they will find, in a bed
somewhere, a brother, withdrawing
in fever,
his thin hand fluttering
in final recognition.

SOME MORNINGS WHEN I WAKE

My hair is straw, filtered
and filched, dulled by the gone
light of the sun
as the earth turns steadily

inward. Then the only
kinship my body
knows is earth

and water, as when,
in the last light of day,
Pinky Fannin's head blushed briefly
to the surface

beside the men searching
where we'd seen him go under,
a red-and-white bobber
disappearing into the lake's secret

dark. Or else
the sound of cicadas will flame the air
in a room
and I will rouse up restless

as perch
and the girl from up the street
again lies down beneath me
and an endless sky

of June. Among the ants
and daisies, our hands

move continuous as cirrus clouds
above us, unnoticed

on the prairie wind. The sun
is as bright as ever shone on Israel
in its first youthful traffic
with the Lord.

We lie on the dry surface
of the ground, breathing easily
as grass. Our sides rise and fall
autonomically. *Out goes bad air,*

in comes good, we say over and over
to ourselves, and pink water drains steadily
down from lips and nostrils, into the light
pooling around us.

On the coffee cup beside me, a wasp
licks and licks its long tongue
over the residue of cream
on the rim, its wings shining darkly back
the glory of light.

DOWN THE MANY STEPS OF LIGHT

Suppose, years later, bananas
grow cheap, oranges roll
like Christmas

into your hands:
the nod of the day
toward you, its hat uplifted
in salute . . .

Will it all then
change, the playback alter itself
like approved
history?

And what of those remembered
shapes, that unchanged flux
of sky?

—the glancing fall of light
on a roof, a sister bathing
and bathing, as in a dream, your eyes,
a gate hanging always open

somewhere else

SOMETIMES MUSIC RISES

Above the snuffle and scurry
of one's own
minor blood, the neck-snapping thunk
a grouse makes as it startles up
into a window, its fanned
tail feathers quivering
with color—brown, ocher, russet—
the driftwood it lies beside smoothed
by rocks
to the curve of a bird's wing.

Or, on earth personal
as breathing, a garage leans
back through summer
toward the sound, not
of saw and axe
in the act of tree fall,
but of wood bees droning
above the private
gloom everyone who slumps
suddenly to the floor
turns into.
"Is it true?" a father asks
in disbelief,
and wood dust falls
from the rafters like denials
of the future.

And what if today someone you
named lingers
beside a stream

and hears, in the great
silence around her, cold
water promising nothing
but itself, the curve
her arm makes among the rocks
a mere accident
of time and weather?

IT IS THE MIDDLE OF THE
NIGHT AND I AM AWAKE

Again, listening to the tumble
and glide of small animals
between the floors. Chipmunks?
Flying squirrels? White-
footed mice? Like the mind

they are nocturnal and gnaw
themselves awake, in spite of warmth
that seeps in through boards smoothed
and varnished with permanence. In the dark,
we are creatures light-years distant

from ourselves.
And lives that reflected the light
decades ago last finally
into sight, voices
that were swirled away

into the great blue quiet
now vibrant
in our ears. *Wayne,*
is they Mickey Mouses
in there? We stand in the dirt

beside the school bus,
the cardboard pencil box in my hand bright
with the Walt Disney promise
of Christmas. We are seven years old.
And for this long January moment the world

she imagines shines back
in unequivocal red

and blue and green and yellow.
In the clear air
that surrounds us, all words

are still possible.
I wonder if she would think me foolish
now, worrying, all these years
later, about the answer
I would give her,

and about the way children down the road
from us grow up and go out
at night sometimes and break
the bones of old people, primary colors
leaching steadily away to mere stains

on a wall, on a dress, on some saved page.

OF DESIRE

The voluptuous way the trees
spring back to leaf each year
on cue, each hue
of green turning us back
toward some first knowledge

of light, the gradual curve
down skin and hair
to the creviced dark our dreams
enter into like wild
guesses . . .

                Now,
in a single tree outside my window,
this palette of birds, brilliancies the sun
threatens every moment to swirl
up into the air like flowers

in flight: gold
and purple finches,
on silver branches daubs
of cardinal
and black, chestnut
and yellow, bright

cerulean against all that vacant
sky the earth
yearns up to.

QUANTUM

I

We set railroad ties in the trench
we dug beside the flower beds
this morning
and shake them firm
on their new bed,
dents from an earlier generation of gravel
now turned up
        to the sun.
The heat today is like the burst
from an exploded star, past
becoming finally
present, our own bodies red
with distance.

II

There are no clouds in this blue sky. The days
spin away so slowly we are like cows,
ruminating green in summer dazzle.
Wherever we look, houses shine back
light, and the sharp whine of flies
veins the afternoon air. Pulse
and pulse.
        Can there be end
to these endurings? Can
the pure color that fills
long miles within us be,

in an instant,
scattered forever?

III

Suppose, years into the future,
one should come upon a man grieving
as over a lost child,
the moaning of trees in the wind a voice
for one who cannot weep.
                             Will it then
happen, consequence on consequence,
that a hand will wave to him
out of the shadows,
like a summons,
and, in that moment of perception,
call him at last
to a gathering among flowers
                             in a meadow,
the afternoon settling always
into the astonished O
of its briney cask?

AGAIN . . .

          morning has arrived
                    like a question,
birdcalls all querulous
          and rising,
                    trucks
on the highway to the south of us
          searching
                    through the gears
toward a place of indecision,
          True/False, True/False . . .
                    True faults
of the mind,
          in time: forgetting
                    and remembering.
Kansas.
          Early morning.
                    The streets yellow dust
in the sunlight,
          backyards stretching themselves
                    full length
between the fences.
          And again my friend and I
                    rise up from sleep
on the hard bed
          of a wheat truck,
                    certain
and supple
          in the day's low promise:
                    the dry smell of grass
and chaff
          along the ditches,
                    the blue shirt of sky

hung out on the line to fade
        toward white,
                flies humming dark
in the cab doze of afternoon,
        10,900 mornings
                ago.
And the people I saw there,
        eating eggs,
                stepping down
from a porch,
        lifting a small piece of cloth
                to the cheek—
do they still,
        rain time or sun time,
                wonder
under the prairie dirt,
        whether they too will push,
                some spring,
their dark way back
        to the surface,
                eyes
viridescent in the changed
        light, wind
                filling their mouths again
with each other's name?
        Again
                morning has arrived
like a question,
        a woolly worm striped
                black
and amber, back
        with its secret knowledge
                from the other side.

II

TONGUES

A certain reticence to speak
out into silence may honor,
it is true, the fluent
mysteries that carve
spaces for us out of air.
But of itself such
niceness is nothing more
than finches, carnelian and slight
against the morning snow.

For while a small inclarity
of light may any moment winter
the mind to stillness,
inevitably someone
in the room will start
to colonize the air
with thoughts as swerveless

as bombers. Ships
will declare
to the circumambient waters
of the earth some bold
plan, and entire nations
of people will strike out

along a line as confident as
red sails in the sunset.
Meanwhile the tongue-
tied brain courses and

courses the narrow channels
of imagination

and memory, but sees
always only dark
green light filtering down
through matter dispersing
above and around us, lovers
waving out of the depths like undulate
grass.

*

And what appeal can be made
from this?
Field mice will gather
anyway beneath a wood pile
the scraps temporary
warmth can be held in, and,
in the steady seep
of cold, dream,
perhaps, like you,
of a system closed,
finally, and made safe

from error: the facts
in, truth
discoverable, the familiar
smells of one's own
body a rainbow
night knows the promise of.

*

And even if someone
should sometime gather to himself

a great pile
of whispers and outcries,
sifted and yellowed
among feathers recumbent
with alteration, and then,

on a sudden, know
the sure presence
of false judgement
at, say,
one avoidable Sarajevo
of human congress

(the way a hawk
in a high wind folds
for an instant
its wings and hangs
motionless in the rushing air),

                         still,
on a February plunge
of ice and wind, hand-
split logs will, in a moment, lift
above us and,
among the sticks and mud and daubs
of man-made fibers, show

again the small
familiar figures waving
handkerchiefs on the shore,
their voices tattering
in the wind those sad
forgotten tongues.

NAGS HEAD

Now the day smells
like the loss of old navies.
At the water's edge, children dart in
and out among plovers and
sandpipers for bright wreckage,
rolled beneath their feet.
Everything, they say, comes ashore
at last.

*

Imagine a horse and lantern
moving through a dark so deep
the sand turns water
in your eyes.
Sails beat the night air like the wings
of some great moth. All
the sound of the air is the roar of
water, waves breaking and driving you
down, until gravel is the only
sky, and your ears fill up
with breakage.

*

We are stranded here for good
or ill. Ask wherever lights seem to move
along the beach.
No one knows the way back
from here. Tomorrow, in bright sunlight, gulls
will lift

above the smell of morning, and offshore
dolphins will cruise steadily north
and south like vacationers,
looking for a way out.

BEFORE DIVORCE

Sometimes, in those years, I escaped
into the hills that surrounded us, drove
until even the dirt roads ended, finally,
up against a wall

of trees, then walked the morning sun
up over pine and fir and aspen, up
until light reddened
in wild strawberries along the banks
of the St. Vrain River

and entered, suddenly, the deep clarity of water
like fish flashing to the bottom
among shadows of boulders large as a house
full of darkness.
Some things are dangerous

to do alone:
go swimming, run a chainsaw,
be married,
fish a fast mountain stream, miles
from any road.

                    It often comes down to just
this: your only remaining
ginger quill, your last chance
to salvage something
of the day your life is

is tangled on a cable angling high
up to rocks above the river, a long

hand-over-hand walk
above the bright water.
I was lucky. Hours later,

long after the day's last light had withdrawn
from the earth, and trees, beneath the pinholes
of stars, had vanished
into the hillsides,
I walked the uncertain trail back

to where I started,
the night so still my own
breath sounded like the wakeful
breathing of unhappiness
in bed beside me.

NOVEMBER

Sky this morning the color of
brains, a bird feeder swinging
and swinging from each launch
of chickadee, titmouse, nuthatch
into the approaching
cold. In the rising wind
the bare trees coil and leap
in place, their long
roots stretching beneath the curve
of hill to strands so
fine they might be hair, waving
and tangling in the intimate slow rhythms
dirt and rocks and darkness
dance to.
       Next week
Thanksgiving, and almost everyone I
love is somewhere else
on the earth.
       A redbellied
woodpecker bangs a tall
poplar and then listens
for a message. I too
press my ear against the creased
bark and hear
the deep swish swish of blood
inside my head.

ON ALL YOUR FINGERS

The pale face of a woman
near the porch in moonlight. Somewhere
around that house hollyhocks
should be blooming, red
as promises. But in this
white light they are dark
as weeds, as her eyes
turning away toward something you still
can't see. Darker
and darker. Fire turning back
to coal.
From behind you the single
plunk of a cowbell, shifted in sleep.
Count this too.

AND WHAT SHALL WE GATHER TO US

Here beside the broad,
majestic Susquehanna?—mile
after mile beside the highway
north, curving us
into islands that rise
out of layered mists above the water
like signs.
                    Like invitations.
Farm for Sale, for instance,

beside another highway, another time.
Always the shared hope: tidy fields, white houses
bubbling up inside the car
like artesian wells
our father knew of—lives
dreamed in dust
and heat, in backyards and
pigpens, in meadows blooming
with broken glass.

Shards and slivers.
Inevitably the mind shatters
at some missed curve, sharp edges rainbowing
the morning light—in grass,
in puddles beside the road. Together
we all crowd around the shock
of it, rehearse details
of the loss, finger,
perhaps, in the souvenir privacy
of our pockets, the torn edges,

the thin sheet of plastic
between layers of glass,

the way we disappear
into ourselves
like Indians, silent as trees
in Nebraska.

*

The farther we go the nearer we come
to something. Every glade, every meadow, every green
draw we come to . . : daffodils
drooping their yellow assertion of April
toward the sogged earth
we keep sinking back to,
in Ohio Oklahoma Montana

The Via Romana . . .
                        As when a child,
barely old enough to talk,
sits on your lap and, smiling, says,
Shall I tell you how I do two
doors? First, I shut the door the world
is outside of,
then, upstairs,

the door I live behind.
                        In a dream, of course,
you would now kiss his cheeks
and lips, know again the chambering salt our lives
taste of, late
and early, feel yourself sliding
already out of your arms and away

31

from the infinite yearning
your body surrounds,

into that inward life we always hunt for
words for.

*

Oh, when Ernest Clelland's small house burned
all the way to the ground
one night in February, miles
through the lightless dark
from anywhere anyone could
have awakened from, the only
other eyes that brief light
shone in were his mules'
near eyes, the others already seeing nothing

but empty hillside. Beyond
the field the trees
stood up into the dark
like unseen smoke. Curve
after curve the road repeated
its one message: Nobody.

                    The durance
and endurance our lives are,
Keats tells us—all
soulmaking. Lumps of melted glass
turned over and raked out of warm ashes, blue
and pink and yellow in the afternoon light.
Small piles of belongings stacked
just beyond the scorch line
on the grass. Mothers in groups
holding our hands and weeping

beside the cars, our fathers
putting their large hands into their pockets
and taking them back out
again, empty
as the space a house stood in, its walls
holding inside themselves the smell
of yeast bread rising and baking
through long afternoons
of winter and summer, spring and fall,
butter churned fresh from cream Mrs. Clelland and I
skimmed from milk in the low kitchen, her great bosom
pillowing me to sleep
in the rocker beside the stove,
the soul growing, filling the walls
behind the door, holding these times, these people,
these walls, changeless and changed
forever.

*

Then one morning we look up and clouds
hang above the poplars like negatives
of leaves already fallen.
                    Frost-heave
and leaf-fall underfoot, the earth with its slow
drum roll beneath the trees, the wind
folding and folding the day's small flags . . .

And we listen for a sound, a voice
within us, its small arm lightly circling
our neck: *Shall I tell you how I do two doors?*

And the sound, like a cry, rises from the roses.

NAMING THE WINTER

As far as I can see
the wood's a harbor, the trees
all dark anonymities against the snow:

white oak and elm and sassafras and linden,
pin oak and hickory, sugar maple
and sweet gum, nameless masts

and spars above an ocean of white, wind
along the surface whipping up and curling
the snow back

in light spray
above all those forgotten
ships, sunken in the earth.

Beneath its glazed surface the tangle
twigs and sticks and lives make
jumbles

to obscurity. Aspen.
Ash. Red maple. Rock oak.
Robert. Margaret. James. Louise.

AND IF SOMEONE . . .

1.

It all, science tells us, varies
and depends. And nothing rises
of its own weight merely.
Hummingbirds, hanging
and hovering in the air
like flowers, bear,
on their slight bodies,
a freight of hopes more lush
and florid than the vast
forests of South America
they fly back to.

Through the rush and blur of wings
you can just make out the figure
nestled in a hammock,
summer air continuous
around her, the rhythmic rise
and fall of her breast a pulse
in your temples. And there,
in the intense light beyond
these cabined memories, someone straightens
from the waist-high lip
of the well, like a father,
and the tin dipper raised
to his mouth drips steadily
down into the certain
and obscure dark.

2.

It is probably best to make up your own
memories, to imagine again
the sweet labial touch
of skin, lightened and curved
by hair and shadow.
For you will picture anyhow
the way cows sometimes in spring
would fall,
moaning, to the earth,
the red-and-white mass of

blood and hair stuck fast
in the monstrously-stretched slits
your dreams were circled
by. And you will still likely
draw your hard, adolescent body up
out of a spring-fed creek
into the whisper afternoon sunlight
makes, and then, in a rush
of something more than surprise
and fear, drive again
and again your fist into the smashed
head of the snake
that suddenly stares from the bank
back at you.

And if someone now beside you
in the bed calls
Oh, look! It's a hawk!
turn with her to the window
and see it
beating up from the tree tops
just outside, the unseen air

warming and rising
above bent-weed and toothwort,
above may-apples and elderberries,
plantain and honeysuckle,
and the hundred other
densities of green,
where blow flies come
and press their ardent mouths
again and again to the soft
and cooling flesh
of a rabbit.

III

THE DAY ROGER CLOUD
KNOCKED MONTE ELAM OVER
THE RIGHT FRONT FENDER OF A CAR
ACROSS THE STREET FROM WEBSTER
JUNIOR HIGH SCHOOL

Maybe I'd been to the library
already, for more of the stories that took me
away from the one-room apartment
I had to set up a cot in the corner of
each night when we went to bed,
my father and mother released,
for a time, into another

corner, from the factories and confusion war-time
had brought them to.
Maybe I had books in my hand as I stood there
on the sidewalk, still innocent
as the sign we put up on the front of the house
lest my brother come home unexpectedly
from the war and miss us

in this strange place: *Homer Dodd*
521½ (in the rear). The afternoon,
I remember, was still, at that time,
bright, like the eyes of the kids
who trailed across the street behind them,
that spring of 1945,
wild, expectant, afraid.

Does the permanent record of that moment show,
I wonder, a truck

full of Mrs. DeGraffenreid's pies
passing, like a vision, out of our lives?
And does the bell of a streetcar packed
with the swing shift for Boeing ring
in the ears of a woman whose thigh

rocks beneath the hand of a marine who is not
the husband home at last
from the Pacific? Could it be possible
those images are rising up even now
before astonished eyes thirty-eight
light years away,
like a sudden row of lumps

on a forehead, or a brief telegram in the afternoon?

DRIVING THE SCHOOL BUS

At this hour we are still
the only ones on the road.
And my father drives us
into light that rises
from the earth like
birdsong, like green
cornfields. Farther
along these ruts moments
so perfect I will remember them
forever wait, like passengers,
beside the road.
In bright sun Holsteins
crop and chew and never think
once about the grass
we turn into.

                    This
is the world as we first
find it, early
in light blackberry bushes
bloom white in.
And these
washboard roads run straight
to the heart of the matter: Some
daybreak many twisting years
later, the sky will open
out like the flute
of a thrush, and I won't,
for a moment, know
whether I am the small boy standing
beside the driver, or the certain route

the road always takes through the mind
of my father, his eyes still blue
and large
in this abundance of light.

LOVE POEM AS MEDITATION

As when Thales of Miletus, convinced
always of the one thing, climbed,
by night, to a peak overlooking the Aegean,
breaking into bright flashes of starlight
on the shore, and watched
the moon fail itself daily
like a flaw
in the mind . . .
                    At night, even now,
in Wisconsin, or on the flat
plains of Kansas, while the prairie sunset still
reddens the horizon
of memory, something can
splash so loud in the dark
the mind, as if on a hill
jutting toward the sea, hears
fish, and so manages to hold everything
together.
                Or perhaps,
on waking, we hear a note
plain through the morning
air. *Bird,* we say, or *Beauty,*
or utter a certain name
we recognize each other
by. The moon, let's say,
holds then the sky
in perfect fullness. Every
word the mouth shapes is some-
one, somewhere.

GLACIER TRAIL, RAINBOW TROUT

Here, on this boulder lapped by snowmelt,
           we can see
     all the way to the gravelled depths
       the bend makes, sunlight
   rippling the surface like breath
        upon the water.

Nine, ten months of the year
     snow piles into this narrow cut
           between rock faces,
   until spruce trees seem
         mere dip sticks
     to measure it with. Still,

new growth is bright
   on the tips of branches,
        and flowers
     splash this black sponge
of earth with all the colors light
       is capable of.

Even before I see them
   I see them, hanging
        and darting in
  fluid sunlight, their sides
     long blossoms
      below us.

We are not fishing, but I speak to you
       of flies,
   how sometimes one tries

to match the hatch of insects
on the water.
And even as I speak

It happens: the stream's surface swarms
into the air
in dots and puffs of buff
and bone, and fish,
as if in illustration, leap
and gulp

this moment into even fuller
life.
Around us are other
signs: trees fallen and rotting
on the earth, shoes cracked and curled
underneath an overhang

of rock, granite blocks no one has ever
seen our
figures in. But as we look down
into the cold beneath us,
your hair like mica
in the bright sun,

I feel
whatever we, at this moment,
are is permanent
in August.

OF RAIN AND AIR

All day I have been closed up
inside rooms, speaking of trivial
matters. Now at last I have come out
into the night, myself a center

of darkness.
Beneath the clouds the low sky glows
with scattered light. I can hardly think
this is happening. Here in this bright absence

of day, I feel myself opening out
with contentment.
All around me the soft rain is whispering
of thousands of feet of air

invisible above us.

f

t shapes itself

skin

dow grass, dark
)es—

are how the earth remembers

itself, how it knows time
as sensation. Here,
in clarities of

water, ice-
scarred rocks leap
and tumble

like the newly
born. And rainbows hang
motionless beneath the surface,

caught
in the brightly focused speed
of light.

49

TWO LOVE POEMS

For Joyce

1.

August 3rd

Maple leaves turn
bottom up in the wind
and above them poplars sway
their long trunks,
breathing out the life
we are living.
In a cedar board a wood
bee drives ceaselessly
its small drill,
sawdust drifting down
like pollen. Now,
at midday, the voices
of birds have become low
and distant, whispers
on a pillow: *You*
are my only dream
of flying. I rise
above you, light
as your hair is,
and follow the pure curve
of your body down
to either sleep
or waking. In you
they are always
the same
perfect flight.

2.
But Mostly

I love the shapes your hands
make, mayapples shining
already with next year's green
and pendant fruit. In their
small turnings, a spring
so future its only sounds are seeds
waits in silence.
Each morning when I rise up
with you, the same
song meadowlarks once raised
to the sun in Oklahoma stubble
curves the light
your hands hold up
into the air.

In the days of my body I will
love you the way a small boy
loves the name the world takes
and gives back to him.
And when once again I am leaves
and wind and the sharp
astonishing taste of water
on your tongue,
I will love,
yea, and cherish you
in the perfect cup your hands
will make, lifting me up
to your eyes, your cheeks,
your warm thirsting lips.

MEADOWLARKS

I

Imagine you catch sight of them standing in short grass
in an open field—from the window of a blue sedan
for example. In the morning light they seem to stretch

upward, pale breasts yellowing up
to the sun, heads and necks reaching
and reaching, like people in a crowd trying to see

something. Even from a distance
the flutter in the throat is visible, the one song repeated
like summer.

II

Hand over hand my father walked the guywire to its top
on the pole, the necks of the other men craned
back, their hands uplifted

against the sun. No one else
had managed to stay on
so long. For a moment he hangs

above my eyes like life
suspended. Then hand over
hand he walks the cable back

to earth. And from the railroad cutting
nearby the meadowlarks' song is the bright sound
of the day itself.

III

The thermometer this morning is at zero, the air
like wire in the throat. Each sound
of axe on oak

and ash the color of wheat stubble stuns
the day for an instant
then vanishes

like birds at last light, echoes spreading steadily
among dark branches. Soon
it will be dawn. Already

through the trees the sky
is pink. And in the new
light chips

fly from the axe like birds
returning, gliding their low arc back
to earth.

DEER TRACKS IN MARCH

I

They have stood, in the pale
half-light of morning, only thirty
feet from my bedroom while I slept,
the large, warm bodies poised

above these small points of contact
with the earth, ears
and faces turned
to the sound of our breathing, faint

among the trees. The ripple of skin
along their flanks, their delicate
legs, the occasional
raised foot . . .

II

then the easy movement away

down the slope, like water
over rocks. Oh, everyone remembers
this, knows a summer
day where water pools
among boulders so tall the sky
is exactly overhead, a place time continues
in forever, light

filling your mind with its touch
on every

surface: rock, skin, water, the dark
sedan with its trunk lid

raised. You remember:
a picnic, perhaps, and everyone
present—sisters, brothers, friends,
your father and mother so young

they seem to walk
upon the water you swing out
from the bank and drop to,
there where the river is deep

as dreams. Remember now? the light
underwater dwindling
and changing, the delicate last
brush of hand on sand

and mud. . . . Then someone
pressing and
pressing, as the lovely afternoon slides
toward night, both sides

for air.
         The brief
uncertain patterns
the water makes
in the dirt . . .

III

as farther away now they pause

among the trees
and disappear, their bodies all at once

transparent, the gray,
half-winter light
along the branches.

NOTES

The epigraph is a quotation from Rilke, "The Ninth Elegy," and is translated by Stephen Mitchell.

"Of Butterflies" is for Robert Bly.

"Again" is for Sam Crossland.

"Tongues" makes reference to Sarajevo, Yugoslavia, where World War I began on June 28, 1914, with the assassination of Archduke Francis Ferdinand of Austria.

"And What Shall We Gather to Us" is for Robert Taylor, Jr.

"Naming the Winter" is for Hilary Masters.

"Love Poem as Meditation" refers to Thales of Miletus, 640–546 B.C., who was the father of Greek astronomy, geometry, and philosophy.

"Beside Mill Creek" is for Richard Hugo.

THE CONTEMPORARY POETRY SERIES

Edited by Paul Zimmer

THE CONTEMPORARY POETRY SERIES

Edited by Bin Ramke

J. T. Barbarese, *Under the Blue Moon*
Wayne Dodd, *Sometimes Music Rises*
Gary Margolis, *Falling Awake*
Terese Svoboda, *All Aberration*

BOOKS BY WAYNE DODD

Sometimes Music Rises   1986
The General Mule Poems   1981
The Names You Gave It   1980
Made In America   1975
We Will Wear White Roses   1974